We Need to Win

Written by
Stephen Rickard

ransom

Jeff sails in his boat.

He needs to win.

He aims to keep the quick boats in sight.

2

Gail runs in the rain.

She needs to win.

In the rain, she will get wet feet.
Gail can not jog. To win, she will
need to be quick on the road.

The boat on the right,
the red boat, needs to win.

You need to be fit in this boat.

The men in this boat feel pain.

Kev hangs on the rings.
He needs to win.

He keeps his legs up high.
Will he let go?

Bob and Kim need to win.

Bob and Kim will not get wet, will not need to rush, and will not feel pain.

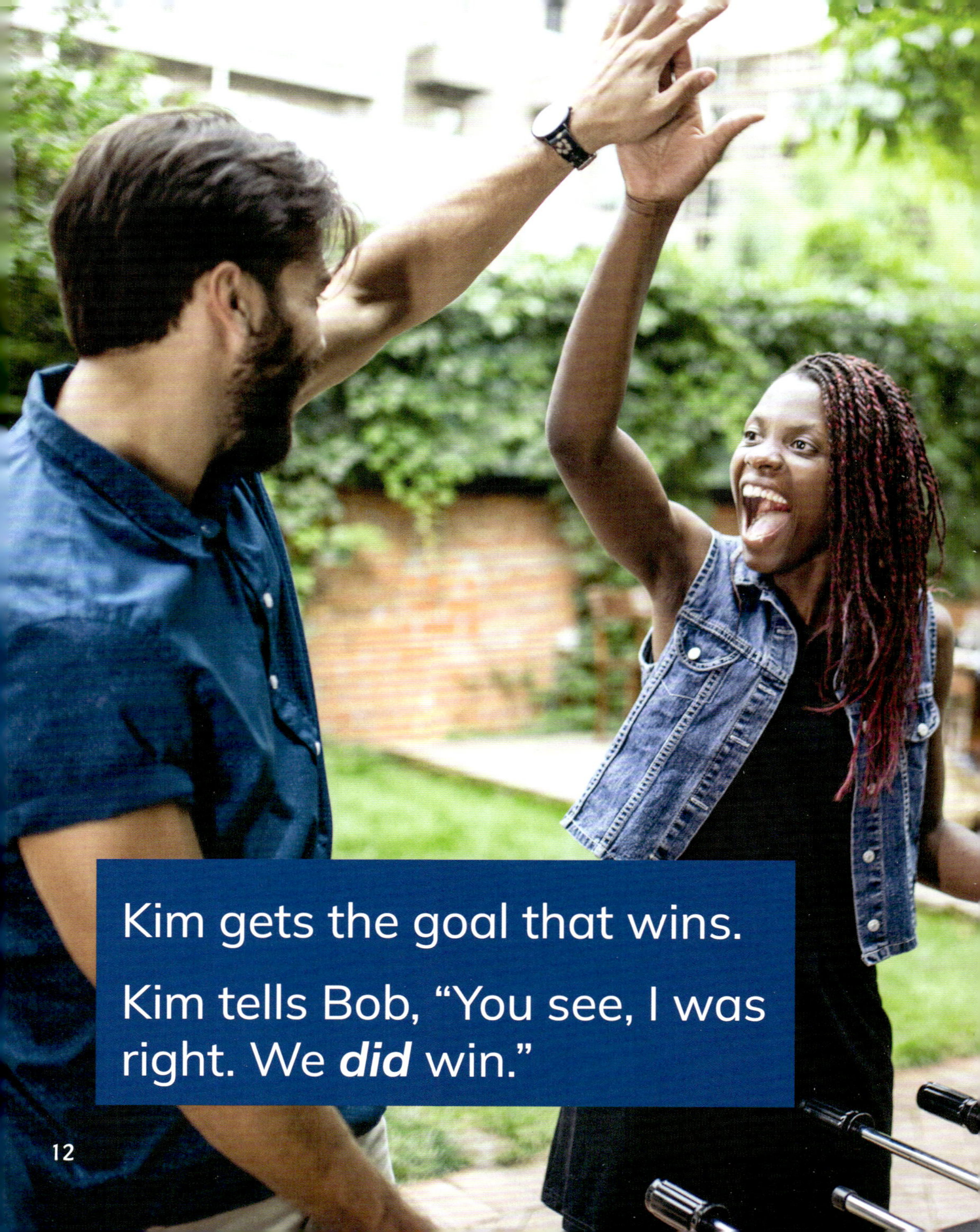

Kim gets the goal that wins.

Kim tells Bob, "You see, I was right. We *did* win."